VOLUME ONE

the Best of the Great Songwriters

SW

Production: Sadie Cook and Carole Staff

Published 1995

© International Music Publications Limited
Southend Road, Woodford Green, Essex IG8 8HN, England

VOLUME ONE
the Best of the Great Songwriters

ANYTHING GOES

Words and Music By
COLE PORTER

© 1934 Harms Inc, USA
Warner Chappell Music Ltd, London W1Y 3FA

4

day ___ An - y shock they should try to stem,_

'Stead of land-ing on Plym-outh Rock, Plym-outh Rock would land on them._

Refrain (*brightly*)

1. In old - en days a glimpse of stock-ing Was looked on as some-thing shock-
(2. When) moth-ers pack and leave poor fa - ther Be - cause they de-cide they'd rath-
(3. When you) hear that La - dy Men - dl, stand-ing up, Now does a hand-spring land-

5

AUTUMN LEAVES

English Words by JOHNNY MERCER
French Words by JACQUES PREVERT
Music by JOSEPH KOSMA

Slowly, with much feeling

Verse (*Slowly ad lib.*)

1. Oh! je vou-drais tant que tu te sou-viennes, des jours heu-reux où nous
2. LES FEUIL-LES MORTES se ra-massent à la pelle, les sou-ve-nirs et les

é - tions a - mis. En ce temps-là la vie é-tait plus belle
re-grets aus - si. Mais mon a-mour si-len-cieux et fi-dèle

et le so - leil plus brû-lant qu'au-jourd-'hui.
sou - rit tou-jours et re-mer-cie la vie.

BLUE MOON

Words by LORENZ HART
Music by RICHARD RODGERS

CLOSE TO YOU (THEY LONG TO BE)

Words by HAL DAVID
Music by BURT BACHARACH

DAYS OF WINE AND ROSES

Words by JOHNNY MERCER
Music by HENRY MANCINI

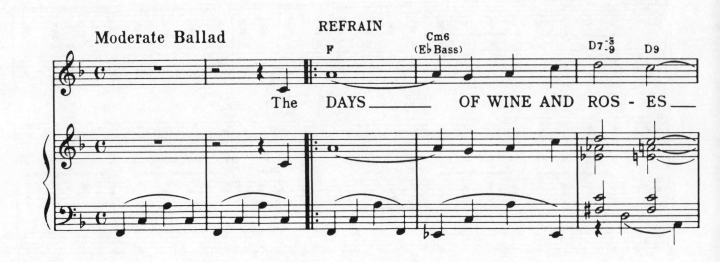

The DAYS _____ OF WINE AND ROS - ES

Laugh and run a - way ___ Like a child at play, ___ Through the

mead-ow-land to-ward a clos-ing door, A door marked "Nev-er - more," That

17

EDELWEISS

Words by OSCAR HAMMERSTEIN II
Music by RICHARD RODGERS

20

GEORGIA ON MY MIND

Words by STUART GORRELL
Music by HOAGY CARMICHAEL

EMBRACEABLE YOU

Music and Lyrics by
GEORGE GERSHWIN and IRA GERSHWIN

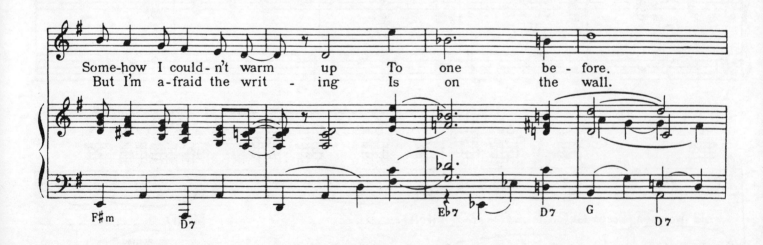

26

REFRAIN (*Rhythmically*)

EV'RY TIME WE SAY GOODBYE

Words and Music by
COLE PORTER

I GOT RHYTHM

Music and Lyrics by
GEORGE GERSHWIN and IRA GERSHWIN

REFRAIN *(with abandon)*

IF EVER I WOULD LEAVE YOU

Words by ALAN JAY LERNER
Music by FREDERICK LOEWE

IF I LOVED YOU

Words by OSCAR HAMMERSTEIN II
Music by RICHARD RODGERS

41

42

IT'S ONLY A PAPER MOON

Words by BILLY ROSE and E Y HARBURG
Music by HAROLD ARLEN

48

THE LADY IS A TRAMP

Words by LORENZ HART
Music by RICHARD RODGERS

p - mf
Cm7
Dm7
G7
I get too hun-gry For din - ner at eight,
p - mf
C
Cm7
Dm7
G7
I like the thea-tre but nev - er come late.
C
Cmaj7
C9
F
Fm6
I nev - er both-er with peo - ple I hate,
C
C+
F
G7
C
G7
That's why the la - dy is a tramp.
mf

52

LET'S DO IT (LET'S FALL IN LOVE)

Words and Music by
COLE PORTER

When the lit - tle Blue-bird, Who has nev - er said a word, Starts to sing "Spring, spring;" When the lit - tle Blue-bell, In the

54

MAYBE THIS TIME

Words by FRED EBB
Music by JOHN KANDER

60

PEOPLE

Words by BOB MERRILL
Music by JULE STYNE

ON THE STREET WHERE YOU LIVE

Words by ALAN JAY LERNER
Music by FREDERICK LOEWE

68

For there's no-where else on earth that I would
F7 B♭maj7 B♭dim C9
rath-er be. Let the time go by, I won't
F7 Cm7 F7 Cm Fdim Cm7 E♭m6 D+
care if I can be here on the street where you
Dm7 B♭6 C9 F9 E♭ F7
1 live. I have 2 live.
B♭ Cm7 B♭maj7 Cm7 F7 B♭ G♭6 B♭
mf
p

OVER THE RAINBOW

Words by E Y HARBURG
Music by HAROLD ARLEN

SOMEDAY MY HEART WILL AWAKE

Words by CHRISTOPHER HASSALL
Music by IVOR NOVELLO

76

78

SUMMERTIME

from *"Porgy And Bess"* By GEORGE GERSHWIN, DUBOSE and
DOROTHY HEYWARD and IRA GERSHWIN

STAR DUST

Words by MITCHELL PARISH
French Translation by YVETTE BARUCH
Music by HOAGY CARMICHAEL

STORMY WEATHER

Words by TED KOEHLER
Music by HAROLD ARLEN

Slow lament

Don't know why _____ there's no sun up in the sky, Storm-y Weath-er, _____

Since my {man}{gal} and I _____ ain't to-geth-er, _____ keeps rain-in' all _____ the time. _____

Life is bare, _____ gloom and mis-'ry ev-'ry-where, Storm-y Weath-er, _____

THREE COINS IN A FOUNTAIN

Words by SAMMY CAHN
Music by JULE STYNE

THREE COINS IN THE FOUN-TAIN, Each one seek-ing hap-pi-ness,

Thrown by three hope-ful lov-ers, Which one will the foun-tain bless?

Three hearts in the foun-tain, Each heart long-ing for its home,

There they lie in the foun-tain Some-where in the heart of Rome.

WALK ON BY

Words by HAL DAVID
Music by BURT BACHARACH

WE'LL GATHER LILACS

Words and Music by
IVOR NOVELLO

94

REFRAIN

YOU'LL NEVER WALK ALONE

Words by OSCAR HAMMERSTEIN II
Music by RICHARD RODGERS

98

NEW YORK, NEW YORK

Words by FRED EBB
Music by JOHN KANDER

Printed by
Halstan & Co. Ltd., Amersham, Bucks., England